GOVERNING IN A SMALL CARIBBEAN ISLAND STATE

JAMES FLETCHER

To my wife Chantal and my mother Esmay

I have come to the conclusion that politics are too serious a matter to be left to the politicians.

- Charles de Gaulle

ACKNOWLEDGEMENTS

Many people have helped make this book a reality. My heartfelt appreciation is extended to the group of friends with whom I shared the manuscript and who provided invaluable feedback that helped me to refine the messages I wished to bring across. Each one of you provided a different perspective that added value to the final product.

My sincere gratitude also goes out to my family who have cheered me on and provided the calm centre to which I can always return.

CONTENTS

PROLOGUE

The Caribbean is going through a period of profound political, economic, social and environmental change. The leadership of the countries is grappling with the challenge of defining national identity and maintaining relevance in the face of an increasingly globalised environment. Rapid advances in technology and the pervasive reach of social media and global information have caused Caribbean societies and citizens to become increasingly influenced and shaped by external cultures and attitudes.

Economic conditions have been negatively affected by the loss of preferential access to traditional markets for primary commodities, a crippling global recession and rising national debt. Meanwhile, governments continue to scramble to improve services and upgrade infrastructure to match more sophisticated expectations from electorates that have been seduced into believing everything is possible with a change in administration.

The social fabric of these relatively small societies has been stretched to fraying point by a confluence of factors: an anachronistic education system that does not prepare young graduates for the world into which they emerge; the increasing cost of health care to cater to populations that have become more sedentary and more prone to the negative impacts of chronic non-communicable diseases; and worrying crime levels that are worsened by the influence of drug cultures.

At the environment level, the region has found itself at the front-line of a serious battle against the wide-ranging negative threats of climate change, with scarce financial or human resources to address these challenges. As a result, most of the countries are in perpetual cycles of repair and recovery from frequent devastating hurricanes, floods and droughts.

There have been efforts to develop regional integration systems to help fashion a stronger, collective response to the myriad challenges confronting these island nations. However, for various reasons, these have not always resulted in the requisite coordination of development efforts. Consequently, Caribbean island nations have primarily pursued local solutions to the many common problems that they face.

The onus has remained largely on the governments to solve all the problems. Successive political leaders and politicians have perpetuated the belief that most of the difficulties facing their country have been brought on by the poor governance provided by the opposing party during its term in office. As a result, the electorate is often left with the impression that these problems can be solved simply by a change in the administration.

There is little magnanimity in the political landscape and rarely is there a coming together of forces and efforts, across the political divide, to address the fundamental problems of the country.

Very often, development agendas appear to have been reduced to five-year cycles, aligned with the timing of a general election. While some administrations have had the foresight to articulate medium to long-term national development plans, a change in administration after a general election usually results in a revision or sometimes complete abandonment of this long-term plan. In other words, national development often stops and restarts with every change in administration.

The result is a discontinuous mode of governance and an electorate that has grown increasingly cynical of the intentions of politicians. Unfortunately, there is also a reluctance by many to engage in any activities at the community or national level that can remotely be viewed as political. This must change if Caribbean countries are to mobilize and engage all available human resources to address the serious economic, social, and environmental challenges that they face.

INTRODUCTION

I have been fortunate to see government operate from several different angles. The first was that of a public officer, fresh from completing my post-graduate studies and full of ideas on how I could cause real change in my new ministry. That stint lasted all of four years and resulted in a letter of resignation in frustration at what appeared to be the unwillingness of the senior management of the ministry to change a model that was operating sub-optimally and not producing results.

Three years later, I returned as a permanent secretary, given responsibility for the same ministry I had resigned from a few years earlier. This provided me with my second perspective of government. There, I appreciated the extent of the power that the permanent secretary, the administrative head of the ministry, wielded to make changes in the operations of the ministry.

Four and a half years after becoming a permanent secretary I was given an opportunity as the cabinet secretary to witness in operation the levers of decision-making in government, the cabinet of ministers. In a way, this perspective provided sharper focus, as I got to see the interplay between the work of the permanent secretary and the thinking of the politicians who had the constitutional authority to provide policy direction to that work.

After having completed my stint as cabinet secretary and head of the public service, I was left thinking that really, running a government was not as difficult as many thought it was. With focused, smart leadership, efficiently run systems, effective collaboration, a clear plan, honest and committed ministers, sensible decision-making, and good communication it could be done.

A three-year stint followed at a senior level in the regional public service in the Organisation of Eastern Caribbean States Secretariat. This helped me observe and participate in governance at a different level. I was able to appreciate the value of regional collaboration, functional cooperation, networking and cultivating good relationships with development partners, all of which are critical for effective governance in a small island developing State.

Fortunately, I would be given another opportunity to test my governance theories in a more direct way, five years after leaving office as cabinet secretary, when I was invited to join the cabinet of ministers and given responsibility by the prime minister to exercise general direction and control (according to Section 69 of the Saint Lucia Constitution) over two ministries. This perspective completed my 360-degree view of what it takes to govern in a small Caribbean country. By the time my stint as a minister had ended, I had accumulated more empirical evidence, sprinkled with a fair amount of experience, to allow me to opine on the issue of governance in the Caribbean. It also helped that I edited and produced four election manifestos, served on the executive and national council of the ruling political party and was able to witness the interplay between party politics and government from very close quarters.

This book is a personal reflection, informed by the education and experiences I gathered along the way. It is written for the new prime minister and political leader of the ruling party, because this is where the locus of power resides in our mode of government and this is the person who determines the tone and direction of the administration. There is, however, one caveat. The recommendations in this book apply only if you intend to run an honest, transparent, fair, people-focused, inclusive government that values and makes the best use of indigenous resources. If you have different intentions, you will not find much value in what I have written.

The inspiration for this book was the classic text by Quintus Tullius Cicero, How to Win an Election. In that very enjoyable and informative little book, Quintus Cicero seeks to give practical advice in a letter to his brother Marcus Cicero, an idealist, who in 64 BC was running for the highest office in the republic, that of Consul of the Roman Republic. Perhaps, in the same vein, the information in this book is the sort of advice I would give to a close friend who was seeking to be the prime minister of his or her Caribbean island nation.

The issues covered are not exhaustive. However, they speak to some of the myriad areas that a new prime minister will have to address, starting with a prequel to assuming the position, which is choosing the right mixture of candidates and setting the appropriate tone during the election campaign. The advice provided seeks to create a palatable mixture of two essential ingredients for success - good governance and sensible politics, because the prime minister has two very important goals: to run a successful government and to lead a victorious party at the next general election.

THE CAMPAIGN

When you agreed to accept the nomination to be political leader of your party you understood the enormous implications of that decision. You would now be charged with the responsibility to lead your party, with its proud historical tradition, into the next general election. The hopes and aspirations of your supporters would now pivot on your shoulders.

The tone you set during your period in opposition will send a signal to the electorate about your leadership style and your priorities. Hopefully, you will appreciate the need to articulate clearly and often your plans for the country. You should not focus only on the ills of the present administration. Your goal is to inspire hope in the electorate that a government led by you as prime minister will be empathetic, purposeful, competent, inclusive and successful. Your party should not come across as one that opposes everything done by the government, yet does not provide any information or indication on how or what it would do differently or better if, and when elected. The electorate deserves to know well in advance your plans to grow the economy, strengthen the social fabric of the society, and manage the natural resources of the country. It should not have to wait for the release of your election manifesto, one or two weeks prior to the general election, to find out how you plan to improve lives and livelihoods, and develop the country.

The most important preparation you should make to govern the country is to ensure that you have the correct mix of qualities and abilities in the candidates your party will be presenting to the electorate for its endorsement and election. One of the arguments against our political system is its inability to produce the requisite critical mass of candidates with the ability to represent their constituents effectively and function successfully in a cabinet. Your job as political leader is to inspire capable and honest men and women, who are liked and respected in their respective communities, to want to join you as candidates. You must create an environment within your party that is welcoming of contending viewpoints and diverse opinions. As the political leader you will have to work closely with your party's executive to identify candidates who are able to win their seat and serve competently in the parliament and possibly the cabinet of ministers. The candidate selection process can make you or break you, both pre- and post-election, so take it very seriously.

Your candidates should be persons of integrity. Candidates must be team players who understand the importance of collaboration, networking and communication. A general election campaign is a gruelling period, with ebbs and flows, successes and disappointments. Some candidates will fare better than others, and it will be your responsibility to provide support and direction to the candidates with more difficult challenges, and affirmation and encouragement to those who appear to have an easier path to victory. Your party must operate as a strong, coordinated team, not as a collection of candidates wearing the same colour shirts and sporting the same party symbol, but running disparate and disjointed campaigns.

If you want to convince the electorate of your ability to discharge the important role of governing the country, your party must look the part of a cohesive, competent, serious unit during the period leading up to the general election. It must demonstrate that it is in touch with the concerns of the electorate and the needs of the country and that it has sensible, practicable solutions to address these issues. As political leader, you must set the pace for a focused, professionally executed, people-centred campaign. Finally, while your most important goal and preoccupation during this period must be to secure the victory of your party and as many of your candidates possible, it is never too soon to start a dialogue with your team on how you will govern when elected. There are many examples of parties that have appeared efficient and prepared during an election campaign, but totally clueless and hapless in government. You do not want this to be your fate.

THE VICTORY

The general election results became obvious a few hours after the polls had closed. The long days and sleepless nights of campaigning in every constituency around the island, the countless meetings of your election strategy committee and campaign teams, the meticulous training of your agents, the constant deployment of canvassers, the diligent coding and recoding of voters' lists, the numerous times you had to intervene to calm tempers, the occasional anxieties over payment of expenses and the availability of campaign paraphernalia and resources, and the frequent engagements with the media to ensure that your campaign messages were getting out to the electorate, were not in vain. Your party had won the general election. The electorate had restored your faith in them and confirmed your belief in the righteousness of your positions. Your opponent had conceded, and you had addressed the country on the national television and radio stations, streamed live on social media, declaring victory and thanking the people for their support and the confidence they had reposed in you and your party.

Then came the countless congratulatory telephone calls from members of your team, family and close friends, and even some totally unexpected well-wishers. By the time you were through answering the phone calls and responding to countless text messages, it was well past midnight. You had driven home, knowing that henceforth, your life would change irreversibly. But this is what you had prepared for, worked hard for, from that fateful day when you accepted the nomination of the delegates from your constituency to run for the position of political leader at your party's convention. Now you hoped that what would follow would unfold just as you had pictured it over a thousand times in your head.

The first order of business the morning after the victory is to make the arrangements for your swearing-in. You must inform members of your immediate family, your closest friends, the candidates of your party, the senior members of your party and your campaign team of the time for your swearing-in ceremony. You should ensure that the diplomatic corps and the relevant civil society leaders are also invited.

Hopefully, you have already discussed and agreed on your choice for attorney general. In deciding on an attorney general, you are looking for someone who has a good understanding of public law, but also someone with a proven track record in court. Remember, the attorney general is not only the chief legal advisor to your government, but also the person who will represent your government in any legal proceedings that are brought against it. In your attorney general, you are looking for someone who is firm, is not afraid of speaking truth to power, and has an even disposition. The attorney general will sit in your cabinet and must manage the Attorney General's Chambers and, depending on how you configure your ministries, may also have to supervise the Department of Legislative Drafting.

But, as they say, 'first things first'. You need to prepare a short, inspiring speech for your swearing-in. These will be your first words as prime minister and you must show that you have successfully made the transition from party to country. You should thank everyone and signal your intention to work assiduously on behalf of every citizen and resident. Once you have gone through the formalities, it will be official – you will be the prime minister, with all the authority and responsibilities that come with this position.

THE FIRST WEEK

The most anticipated decision you will probably ever make as prime minister is your first - the choice of people to serve in your first cabinet. Almost immediately the general election results became clear, speculation had started in all corners of the country on who would be in your cabinet. How would you put the portfolios together? Would you keep the combinations that had been used by the previous administration or would you come up with something different? Would you bring in some ministers through the Senate? Who would be your minister for finance? Would you go the way of your predecessors and take that portfolio for yourself or would you give it to someone in your team who had better credentials in economics or finance? How many ministries would you take for yourself?

Before you put your portfolios together, you need to get a clear understanding of how the ministries are currently configured. How are the government departments established and where are they located? It would be wise to have someone senior within your team, with knowledge and experience of the operations of the public service but not under consideration for a cabinet position, who will serve as your transition manager. Together with your transition manager, your first task as prime minister should be to meet with the cabinet secretary and the permanent secretary in the Ministry of the Public Service to become fully apprised of the current public service landscape. After this meeting, you should have a very clear understanding of how the public service is currently organised and an idea of how your proposed configuration may evolve from the present structure.

Your next set of meetings should be with the permanent secretary in the Ministry of Finance and the commissioner of police. From the former you want a clear snap shot of the state of the government's fiscal position. Are there any issues that require urgent attention? Are there decisions that may have been postponed during the election campaign by the previous administration that can no longer be delayed? From the commissioner of police, you need to get a sense of the national security situation and any serious security challenges. Also, and this may sound harsh, but you need to safeguard the critical government offices to prevent the possibility of any curious post-election migration or destruction of files and other important documents. The Office of the Prime Minister, the Ministry of Finance and the Ministry of Infrastructure (or Works) must be secured.

After you have concluded your meetings you should be clear on what is practicable with your portfolio assignments, without causing mass confusion and dysfunction within the public service. This is an important consideration that should not be underestimated. The public service is a large mechanism with many moving parts. You need to understand how these parts function before you set out to rearrange them.

Now it is time to assemble your cabinet. You should resist the urge to design a cabinet based on the strengths of your winning candidates. Your first consideration should be the optimal combination of portfolios to achieve synergies and to give you the best possible chance of governing efficiently and effectively. Having done that, you should then seek to match people to positions.

There are some specialised positions that may require you to bring in cabinet members through the Senate, if the requisite skills do not reside within your successful candidates. Your primary goal should be to put the best persons to head your ministries. This advice also extends to you. If you are not a development finance or economics expert and there is someone within your successful candidates who is better suited for the position of minister for finance than you, then give him or her the portfolio. The prime minister is the ultimate decision maker on where funds are allocated in the budget. You do not derive power from your control of the Treasury; you wield power from your position as prime minister.

FIRST IMPRESSIONS

Your first cabinet should demonstrate that you are serious about putting the country first. It cannot be about rewarding candidates for their loyalty during the election campaign. Later, I will discuss the true role of a member of Parliament (MP), which is to provide the very best representation for the people who elected him or her into office. This is done at the constituency or local government level, not at the cabinet level. This is not to say that the two roles cannot intersect. They can do so successfully, and I have seen examples in both major political parties in my country. But just as often, depending on the individual or the portfolio, they do not coexist effectively, and you need to give your MPs and your cabinet the very best chances to succeed.

The practice of chopping and changing portfolios with every change in administration or every cabinet reshuffle is counterproductive, disruptive and inimical to the smooth functioning of government. Therefore, my advice would be that you deliberate carefully on the optimal configuration of portfolios to allow for the efficient and cohesive operation of your administration, and, having established these portfolios, do not make any major changes to them again. This may not be popular advice because many prime ministers see the loss of ability to rearrange ministerial portfolios with every cabinet reshuffle as a restriction of their powers. However, if you are serious about governing, you will place a higher premium on efficiency and effectiveness than on designing and changing portfolios to match the needs or hide the weaknesses of individuals.

I am not an advocate of trying to reduce the number of ministries to some single digit number just because it supposedly demonstrates you are running a lean government. There is not a linear relationship between the complexity of governance and the size of your country or its population. It is difficult to give some portfolios the attention they require if they are lumped together with other unrelated agencies. Conversely, creating several small portfolios and populating them with ministers just so that you may fulfil the cabinet ambitions of all the members of your team is bad governance.

Ministers should be given distinct and direct responsibility for their portfolios. There should be no ambiguity over who is responsible for a sector. Effective collaboration between and among ministries should be a goal of your administration and this is best achieved through the functioning of standing cabinet sub-committees, which report on a regular basis to cabinet.

In deciding on the people to fill ministerial positions, you need to find individuals who have the capacity to understand the sectors for which they have been assigned responsibility. Running a ministry is a difficult, complex and time-consuming undertaking. The minister must be able to (i) motivate others, (ii) inspire confidence, (iii) communicate effectively, (iv) consult and learn from his or her professional and technical staff, (v) make decisions on a timely basis, and (vi) articulate a vision and possess a passion for the areas under his or her purview. Most importantly, your ministers must be honest, of sound mind and unimpeachable character. This last set of qualities is critical and anyone who is deficient in these areas should not be given responsibility to head a ministry and sit in your cabinet.

You have a few more important positions to fill - your senators, the Speaker of the House of Assembly and the President of the Senate. The latter two persons should have a good understanding of the law, be well versed in parliamentary procedure, fair, firm, decisive and of even temperament. Your senators should be selected from competent, honest people who support the policies of your administration and who can be expected to make a positive and meaningful contribution to parliamentary debate.

THE FIRST 100 DAYS

There is a ritual surrounding the first 100 days in office of a new administration. Your performance in your first 100 days is used to gauge the tenor of your administration. Will you be bold or conservative? How will you treat with the programmes of the previous administration? What approach will you take with the persons appointed by your predecessor?

From the outset, allow me to confess that I am not a fan of 100-day agendas that focus on fulfilling manifesto promises. I believe they serve very little purpose, save for initial public relations that suggest you are getting work done. Unless you are a returning administration, your first 100 days will be spent, or should be spent, managing the transition from election campaign to government, settling your cabinet, making appointments to the boards of directors of statutory corporations, understanding the state of the country's finances, coming to grips with the on-going programmes being executed by your respective government agencies, introducing your administration to development partners and finalizing the management of your overseas missions.

Choosing the persons to sit on the boards of your statutory agencies is an important decision, which must be handled with care and deliberation. Chairpersons and board members should be chosen from persons who have the requisite competence and integrity to discharge the governance functions of these boards. The role of political parties is to seek to remain in power and this consideration should never be lost on a new administration. Therefore, it is understandable that your administration would wish to appoint chairpersons of statutory agencies who are competent and honest, but also sympathetic to the policies of your party. However, this should not extend to the point where it prevents capable citizens who have the right skill sets from serving your administration simply because they are not known supporters of your political party. Also, it should not cause you to place unskilled and poorly suited persons on boards simply because they support your party. Dividing the country's human resources into government and opposition supporters after a general election means that you will always be robbing your administration of the skills of a significant percentage of the population - those who did not vote for you or those who you perceive do not support your party. Caribbean countries are too small and the human resources too limited for the nation to be denied the services of competent individuals simply because they do not support the ruling party.

During the first 100 days, you should organize a retreat for your cabinet. Most of your ministers will probably be new to the operations of government and may have never worked in the public service before. This retreat should be facilitated by an external, objective, non-political agency, with experience and competence in hosting such a session. It should cover topics such as fiscal management, public service management, budget preparation, the role of statutory agencies, the role of the minister and the permanent secretary, parliamentary procedure, emotional intelligence, crisis management, effective communication, etiquette and protocol. This retreat should be repeated later in the life of your administration. The second iteration will allow for a refresher and reinforcement of things previously learned, this time informed by the experiences of your team in government. It will also give you an opportunity to do a stock-take of your performance as a government.

There is a tendency among new regimes to stop or dismantle projects that were established by their predecessor, without assessing the utility of the respective initiatives. This does not make for good governance. During the first 100 days, you should initiate an objective review of any questionable capital projects, before a decision is made about their fate. Similarly, the practice of renaming existing projects simply to claim ownership of them is trivial and suggests a government that is more interested with show than substance. You should avoid these instincts at all costs.

Your appointments to the prime minister's inner administrative team should also be made in the first 100 days. Your administrative attaché should be an energetic, intelligent, research oriented individual, with good speech writing abilities. Your press secretary should be an experienced media practitioner, fluent and comfortable in all media, particularly social media. This person should not be confrontational and must understand that their role is to develop positive and productive relationships with the media, locally and externally, to promote the work of the prime minister and the government.

You should not underestimate the impact that the election campaign had on you and your candidates. It was a period of frenzied activity, high tension, acrimonious debate, long days and sleepless nights, and many hours spent on the road criss-crossing the country. As one veteran of several campaigns explained to me, "an election campaign is gruelling and combative, it takes a serious toll on the body and mind of all concerned, particularly the political leader. The debilitating effects of a campaign show in the faces of the candidates for weeks after the general election has ended". You should try to create some opportunities for unwinding and relaxation for your candidates and your campaign team after the campaign has ended. It is very important to include the candidates who were not victorious in this exercise. It is easy for losing candidates and campaign managers, who were part of a close-knit team during the campaign, to feel left out and abandoned during this period.

It can be difficult sometimes to transition efficiently and smoothly from the high adrenaline, contentious atmosphere of an election campaign to the calmer, more structured environment of government. Often, there is a carry-over of hurt feelings and a desire to 'get back' at certain people for unfair accusations or negative actions during the campaign. You must guard against using your new position of power and authority to address campaign grievances. You should impress on your team the need to adopt a conciliatory and magnanimous posture. It will be difficult, but it is a necessary part of the healing that must take place for your team and the country if you are to govern effectively. There is nothing wrong in defending your integrity and correcting any untruths or misconceptions that may have been circulated during the election campaign, but you must also understand that the campaign is now over. You won the general election. You and your team must filter out the residual background noise of the campaign and focus on running the government.

THE CABINET OF MINISTERS

Your ministers do not need to be subject matter specialists in the areas for which they have been given responsibility. In fact, in some instances, the subject matter specialist minister may cause more harm than good by not being able to resist the temptation to insert him or herself in the day-to-day operations and management of the ministry. I have seen this happen and the results are invariably bad. Your ministers must have the competence to understand the operations of the sector(s) under their purview and the capacity to interact constructively with professionals in and out of the public service to develop policies that contribute to the development of their sector. They should be able to deliberate intelligently on the policy options presented to them and determine whether the decisions they are contemplating will contribute to the positive development of the citizens of the country.

However, regardless how competent your new ministers may be, it is more than likely that they will have very little experience with, or knowledge of the operations of the public service. You should not underestimate how large a challenge this can be. In addition to the previously recommended retreat of your cabinet during the first 100 days, which will provide much-needed exposure to the basic elements of life as a minister in the government, you should ensure your ministers are given the tools necessary for their success.

There are certain laws and procedures with which every minister of government must become closely acquainted if he or she is to function effectively. The Constitution of the country is the first and most important of these. The Finance Act or the legislation that establishes the procedures and provisions for the management of public funds runs a close second. Because every minister is responsible for a department of government and is expected to exercise that authority through a permanent secretary and the public service apparatus, the laws and any procedures that govern the management of the public service should be explained in detail to each minister. The attorney general and the cabinet secretary should be assigned the responsibility for organizing this training.

Your ministers must understand the limits of their authority and the extent to which they are able to 'exercise general direction and control' over their ministry, which is how ministerial authority is defined in many Caribbean nation Constitutions. I have seen situations where ministers have not clearly understood their roles and responsibilities, become involved and sometimes embroiled in public service management matters, and consequently, developed an adversarial relationship with their permanent secretary. I have also witnessed instances where permanent secretaries usurp the role of their minister or repeatedly fail to provide the requisite level of support, and the minister loses all trust in the permanent secretary. On at least two occasions I have had to intervene to mediate a breakdown in the relationship between a minister and a permanent secretary and my experience is that once the trust has been lost, it is very difficult to mend the relationship. This is a situation you should wish to avoid at all costs. If a problem arises between your minister and his or her permanent secretary, it should be addressed promptly, first by your cabinet secretary, then by your public service minister and finally, if necessary, by you.

You are the chairman of the cabinet. It is your responsibility to ensure that your cabinet members operate effectively and efficiently. Therefore, you must keep regular contact with your ministers. Not all ministers are the same. Some are focused and do not need much supervision. They can be depended on to get on with the agenda of your government and require only the periodic assessment to ensure continued congruence between their ministry's plans and the goals of the administration. Others may need more regular encouragement, support and oversight. With these, you should have more frequent, in-depth meetings. Do not underestimate the importance of this responsibility. You must ensure that you allocate sufficient time for this part of your job. Neglected ministers may easily form the wrong impression of your relationship with them. Also, there is the additional danger that this may lead to a chronically underperforming minister, which will reflect badly on your entire administration.

You should agree on clear short-term and medium-term targets and milestones with each of your ministers and this should be done on an annual basis. All your government agencies should be made to establish objectives and goals at the beginning of every financial year. It is vital that you impress upon your ministers and all your senior managers that you intend to run a results-based administration. Resources are finite and time is limited, so everyone must remain focused on the goals of the government; everyone must be held accountable.

THE CABINET AGENDA

At least once a week, your cabinet will meet to make policy decisions that will determine how the country is governed. You have two options before you as you start your term in office. You can do like many administrations and mandate that every executive question must come to cabinet for a decision. This usually means that applications for concessions from investors, incentives for businesses, scholarships and other training awards must all come to cabinet for consideration and approval. Or you can decide that cabinet should not occupy itself with mundane, routine matters that can best be left to competent senior public officers to decide, guided by clear parameters that have been defined by the cabinet. Instead, cabinet should focus its attention on the serious policy decisions that will determine the direction in which the country progresses.

My experience is that many cabinets prefer the former arrangement, because they believe that it allows them to control most of what takes place in the country. However, the reality is that by allowing such minutiae to dominate its agenda, the cabinet robs itself of the time and the ability to deal with serious policy and governance issues. Your cabinet should set and publish clear guidelines and procedures for the processing of scholarships, concessions, incentives and licenses and leave these and other routine matters to your ministers to address, informed and assisted by the professionals in their ministry. In some instances, there may be a statutory requirement for cabinet to be the final authority on what should be a routine decision. Where this is the case, you should cause the relevant legislation to be amended to relieve your cabinet of this unnecessary burden. Every quarter, the ministers who have been clothed with the responsibility for adjudicating on matters that previously came to cabinet, should present a report to the cabinet secretary providing details on when and how this authority was exercised and the cabinet secretary should compile this information into a report for the cabinet. You will find that investors and everyone concerned will have much more faith in the system when they know up front what they are entitled to and that these decisions are being made purely on merit.

Your cabinet should focus on the policy considerations that will positively transform the lives of the citizens and place the country on a trajectory of sustained growth and development. You should also organize cabinet's work into sub-committees that focus on the important issues facing the country. There is a practice in our jurisdictions for the cabinet agenda to be determined solely on the basis of the memoranda submitted by ministries, through their ministers.

This is akin to the tail wagging the dog. Your cabinet should be proactive in determining the issues confronting the country, deciding on the policy gaps that need to be addressed, and then directing the relevant government agencies to submit memoranda to cabinet, through their minister, with policy recommendations that will address these issues.

There is a school of thought in some quarters that meetings of the cabinet should never be violated by external bodies. While it is true that the deliberations of cabinet are sacrosanct and must always be shielded from external influence or lobbying, a strict interpretation of this philosophy, in my opinion, robs the cabinet of one of its major levers – the ability to shape and influence decision-making in the country. A cabinet meeting is, and should always be, a formal discussion among the people who have sworn to conduct the affairs of the executive branch of the government impartially and to the best of their ability. However, the cabinet should also avail itself of the opportunity to meet, as and when required, with the public service, the private sector, civil society groups, the trade unions, youth organizations and any other bodies that play a pivotal role in the development of the country.

Consequently, I would recommend that periodically, cabinet engages formally with each of the ministries or key statutory agencies so that the administrative head of the respective ministry or statutory agency can present to cabinet the plans and programmes of the agency and cabinet, in turn, can question the agency on the efficacy of its work programmes. Also, the cabinet secretariat should arrange for meetings with key civil society groups where a frank, constructive engagement may take place on the national development imperatives and a clear understanding reached on the roles of the respective bodies in advancing the development agenda.

The memoranda submitted to cabinet and the deliberations of the cabinet must always remain confidential. However, except for sensitive matters or issues impacting national security, there is no harm in making public the general decisions of the cabinet. Therefore, I would recommend that cabinet directs the cabinet secretary, the information minister or another designated minister to hold weekly post-cabinet briefing sessions, to which the media should be invited. I had this responsibility when I was cabinet secretary and I found the exercise helped to remove some of the suspicions about the workings of the cabinet.

FISCAL DISCIPLINE

A major preoccupation of any new administration is always the financial state of the government and the health of the economy. The pre-eminence of these issues and the fact that the availability of funding determines the government's ability to execute its work programmes and keep its campaign promises are the reason the prime minister often believes that he or she should be the minister for finance. Unless as prime minister you are skilled and experienced in financial management or economics, you should avoid taking the position of minister for finance. Ideally, the minister for finance should be a sound, responsible, strategic manager with a very good understanding of development economics and public finance. Of course, if there is no one within your elected MPs who fits that description, then the responsibility for the Ministry of Finance should fall to you.

You must be reasonable and judicious in how you seek to raise revenue. The option that is most readily available to government to raise revenue is taxes, be these on imports, goods and services, property or income. Therefore, fiscal discipline is very important. The government cannot continue to raise taxes on its citizens and on businesses to satisfy its increasing expenditure needs. At some point, this constrains growth and becomes counterproductive. Neither should it increase its borrowing levels beyond prudential limits as this will negatively impact its credit worthiness and its ability to mobilize loan funding at affordable interest rates to finance its development agenda.

Exercising fiscal discipline will necessitate that you have frank discussions with civil society organizations and with the electorate. It is not everything that the population wants that it can get. Also, and this is often a sobering discovery for many new governments, it is not every major initiative that you promised during an election campaign that you will be able to deliver. The trade unions will be an important partner in this exercise. While always being cognizant of the cost of living, wage increases must also be correlated with productivity and value added. There should be a constructive, continuing dialogue between government and the trade unions on these and related issues.

You and your cabinet should always be focused on the long-term growth and development prospects of the country. Your administration must define the national development agenda. You must establish the national priorities and align spending with those priorities. For example, if it is your goal to provide universal health care to your citizens, and you have embarked on the construction of modern health care facilities, then you will have to invest from the outset in the training of the personnel who will manage and operate these facilities. Importantly, however, you will need to decide very early on how you will finance the operations of the new facilities and the basket of services that you will make available to the population under the universal health care programme. Through all of this, you should communicate clearly and honestly with your citizens so that they are aware of what you are doing and understand the roles that they will be expected to play to make this initiative succeed. It is reckless and irresponsible to embark on new initiatives that will dramatically increase public sector expenditure before you have determined how this additional expenditure will be covered or how the services they will provide can be sustained.

When analysing their debt-to-gross domestic product (GDP) ratios, most governments obsess, understandably, over ways to reduce their debt burden. While this is important, for reasons stated earlier, it should not be your sole preoccupation. Another way to reduce your debt-to-GDP ratio is to intensify your efforts to grow the economy. Incurring debt is not that big a problem if you have the capacity to repay it on a timely basis, without hardship or sacrifice. It sounds simple, but its significance is often lost on many administrations that are desperately trying to fall within the prudential limits set by central banks and international financial institutions.

THE ECONOMY

As the head of government, you must understand clearly the structure of the economy of your country. Is it conducive to achieving sustained growth? Is emphasis being placed in the right places? Are some of the traditional sectors still relevant in an evolving and increasingly complex global environment? Are the services provided encouraging or frustrating investment and economic development?

There have always been one or two major sectors on which national economies of small island developing States depend. Whichever the sector, there are certain issues that restrict competitiveness. Productivity of the work force is one. Dependence on expensive foreign inputs is another. The high cost of electricity is a third. The cost of doing business with government is often a serious impediment to economic growth.

Your task, therefore, in seeking to stimulate sustained economic growth, will be to systematically tackle and address all the issues constraining economic development. It does not matter which sectors you decide will be your primary engines of growth, unless you address these systemic impediments, you will realise sub-optimal results. Some of them, like the cost of imported inputs, will be more difficult to resolve. Here, the prudent application of tax incentives to companies that have demonstrated the capacity to operate efficiently and expand output is one tool that should be used. By providing relief from import duties you can help these companies reduce their production costs. There is, however, a trade-off in government revenue foregone and this must be assessed as part of the cost-benefit analysis that you should undertake.

Fortunately, the problem of the high cost of electricity is soluble, but it will require a clear roadmap for increasing investments in renewable sources of energy and encouraging energy efficiency. If you can drive the price of electricity down to low, stable levels, all your economic sectors immediately and automatically become more competitive and viable.

The cost of doing business with government is a vexing issue for every investor, local or foreign. However, it is one of the more easily solved problems, because all it takes is political will, courage, commitment and a plan. The strategic use of information technology and business process reengineering are effective tools to eliminate unnecessary bureaucracy, shorten the time taken to process transactions and reduce this cost.

Addressing the problem of low productivity of your work force will require constructive and honest engagement with the trade unions. There must be mutual understanding of the importance of this objective and an agreement on how it will be addressed. You must move purposefully to improve the skills of your work force. It is an inescapable fact that our education system is not equipping our current crop of graduates with the abilities and aptitudes needed for this 21st century globally-networked, ultra-competitive, customer-focused, knowledge-based market. You will continue to face problems of inefficiency and sub-optimal economic output if you persist with an education system that is so woefully anachronistic.

You should also explore all viable opportunities to diversify your economy. Information technology services, where the market is global, dynamic and expanding, is one possibility. The creative industries, where young people continue to demonstrate their capacity to create products that are in high demand, many of which can be sold digitally to a global audience, is another potentially lucrative option. You should view your trained labour force as an export commodity and use State infrastructure to find job opportunities overseas for the many skilled, trained persons you cannot absorb domestically. Remittances have traditionally played an important role in the economies of Caribbean countries and should not be ignored by your administration.

THE INVESTMENT CLIMATE

I will confess from the outset that I am not a fan of economic citizenship or citizenship by investment programmes. Although I once argued in favour of one in Parliament, my position has changed significantly. I have read the arguments and I know of the examples where many countries, including developed ones, have used variations of this programme to entice foreign direct investment or attract exceptional intellectual talent. However, it is easier to accept selling citizenship in a country of millions of inhabitants and large land mass, than it is in our small Caribbean island States. I believe that an economic citizenship programme is something you should do only after you have exhausted all reasonable measures to improve the investment climate in your country and attract quality new investments.

If your country already has an economic citizenship programme, you must ensure that it (i) operates with the strictest due diligence checks, (ii) is fully transparent in the manner in which it is administered, (iii) does not cause inflationary pressure on the price of real estate so as to drive ownership of lands out of the reach of locals, (iv) restricts land ownership under the programme to certain defined areas that have been targeted for development, (v) encourages investments in key areas that will redound to the benefit of a wide cross-section of the population, (vi) does not cause your country international embarrassment, and (vii) does not devalue or undervalue what it means to be a citizen of your country.

However, regardless whether you do or do not have an economic citizenship programme, there are certain things you must do to make your country more investor friendly. Foreign direct investment (FDI) is critical for the growth of your economy. It sends a strong signal of confidence in your administration, which does not go unnoticed in the international community. Moreover, it often leads to an increase in construction activity, which is good for employment in the short-term, not to mention the positive long-term effects of the new investment on job creation.

One of the recurring gripes of investors is the frustration of doing business with the public service. The systems are too bureaucratic, repetitive, redundant and time consuming. Additionally, public officers are not trained to deal with investors; they are trained to treat everyone the same way. Therefore, the urgency and alacrity of action that an investor requires are very rarely satisfied by the public service. Many governments have spoken about creating a dedicated agency where an investor can get all applications approved and paperwork processed. Sadly, cabinets are reluctant to repose the necessary authority and power in an investment authority to make these one-stop shops operate effectively. Also, the back-end processes that would allow these investment facilitation agencies to operate seamlessly and efficiently are seldom addressed. Therefore, often it is an idea that has not been allowed to work. Your challenge will be to change the way your public service operates and remove the unnecessary hurdles that investors must navigate past. It should no longer be necessary to send an investor or their agent criss-crossing the public service to stand in lines in several departments to complete multiple forms for various permits or services. The effective use of technology should allow for most of the necessary applications to be completed and submitted online, with all relevant supporting documents, via a secure, dedicated investment or business web portal. Similarly, for local investors or business owners, the government should not require that they go from one government agency to another to collect information that the government already has in its possession, just to resubmit this to a government agency in support of an application. These simple changes can dramatically improve the attractiveness of your country for new investment.

Applications for incentives should not all have to go to cabinet for approval. Every investor should be able to go to a dedicated web portal and access the full range of investment-related services and information, including details on the levels of incentives that are available for each sector and type of investment. In most instances, the parent ministry should be empowered to approve the application on behalf of the cabinet. Fortunately, you have ample examples of best practices in this area in other countries, which you can replicate or adapt to make your systems and your procedures more business and client-friendly.

You should retool your incentives regime so that it becomes a more effective instrument for not simply encouraging new investment in defined areas, but also stimulating expansion in existing viable enterprises. Incentives should encourage investors to do more than the routine.

Finally, do not neglect your local investors in the pursuit of foreign direct investment. Local investors have a vested interest in the growth of the economy and the development of the country. They deserve the same, if not more, support, encouragement and facilitation as your government provides to foreign investors.

HUMAN RESOURCE DEVELOPMENT

Reducing unemployment and creating enduring jobs is a critical focus of every administration, new or returning. Therefore, I have no reason to believe the situation is any different for you as you start your journey as prime minister. What is not often appreciated, however, is the inextricable link between job creation and the education and attitude of your labour force. Consequently, I have linked the two in this chapter.

To be clear, I am not speaking simply about placing unemployed people in vacant positions, because there are seldom sufficient vacant positions to make that big a dent in unemployment. The issue here must be to create new jobs, either in existing sectors or in emerging ones. How do you go about doing this? Well, I assume there is still capacity within your dominant sectors for expansion. This is where your targeted incentives regime will come into play. You should meet with the major stakeholders in these sectors very early in the life of your administration to have a series of frank discussions with them about the support they will require from you to expand their operations. Some of that will come from the changes already discussed that need to be made to stimulate new economic activity. However, there may also be sector-specific adjustments that are required.

If you provide impetus for the development of new sectors like information technology services, creative industries or renewable energy, new jobs will be created that will be very attractive to young people, which is where you probably have the biggest unemployment problem.

Your government should pursue efforts to green the economy. Green economy scoping studies in countries like Barbados, Jamaica, Haiti and Saint Lucia have demonstrated how transitioning to a green economy will benefit Caribbean countries by improving the resilience of their economies, distributing economic benefits more equitably, and more effectively managing ecological resources (United Nations Environment Programme, 2011). For Caribbean countries with fragile but rich and diverse ecosystems, which depend on tourism and agriculture as primary drivers of economic activity, this can be of significant economic and environmental benefit.

As stated previously, the preparedness of your school graduates for the world of work is a major constraint to your efforts to attract new, high quality investments. Many of the graduates do not possess the skills that the new knowledge-based environment requires. I am not referring solely to academic or technical abilities, but also to the important softer skills like communication, networking, the ability to function in a team, self-motivation and conflict resolution. The work environment has become very dynamic. The days of specialising in one area and remaining in it for the rest of your working life are quickly disappearing. The rate at which new knowledge is being produced and the sheer volume of information that is available are staggering. The education system must cater to the concept of continuous learning. Your average school leaver must look forward to several potential career changes before retirement, which will require a new type of literacy, what Alvin Toffler referred to as "the ability to learn, unlearn, and relearn" (Gibson, 1998).

The focus on education must start from the early childhood development period, which coincides with the phase of most rapid brain development in the child (McCain & Mustard, 1999). Inadequate development can lead to significant challenges later. Your education policies must also pay close attention to remediation, so that problems or challenges encountered at the primary levels can be addressed and corrected early. You should ensure that universality of education coverage extends from pre-primary (early childhood) to secondary school levels.

Your education system must recognize that the ability to work across multi-disciplinary and multi-cultural teams is an essential quality for today's employee. Therefore, it must change its approach away from one that rewards single-minded, individual effort to one that also encourages partnerships and teamwork. The education system, at all levels, must constantly preach the gospel of productivity and work ethic. In addition to good grades, students must also be taught the importance of communication skills, punctuality, networking and conflict resolution.

Training of the work force is not the sole responsibility of the government. The private sector has an important role to play in human resource development. Therefore, I would advise that you consult with the private sector and develop mechanisms that will encourage them to invest in the continuous training of their work force.

Finally, and importantly, you should resist the temptation to simplify the issue of job creation to the citizenry. There are serious fundamental elements that militate against the quick creation of the number of quality, enduring jobs you will require to drive unemployment down. Your approach should be to seek to provide short-term relief through the expansion of existing enterprises, while making the more serious and difficult adjustments that will resolve the unemployment problem in the medium to long-term. It is not insurmountable, but it requires a carefully developed plan and commitment.

SOCIAL COHESION

Achieving social cohesion is very important for your success as a leader of your country. Often, governments devote most of their attention to economic growth and development, with a disproportionately small degree of focus on the social sectors. Not only is this misguided strategy, but a breakdown in the social sectors can cause any economic gains to unravel very quickly. It is just as important, therefore, to integrate social planning into national development planning.

The relevance of education and human resource development to the national economy and job creation has already been touched on in the previous chapter. Your education and social services must cater to the differently-abled in the society. It is a sad reality that many governments treat people with disabilities, who make up a larger proportion of the population than we recognize, as second-class citizens. Your school system, from pre-primary to tertiary, must cater to students with disabilities and must provide every opportunity for these students to integrate and receive the same level and standard of education that other children receive.

Proper health care is important but expensive. Consequently, the healthier you can keep your population, the better you will manage the financial burden of health care. Your citizens should not find themselves in a situation where they cannot access basic health services because of economic circumstance. Therefore, the creation of a programme of universal health care, if one does not already exist, should be a goal of your administration. It will create additional strain on government expenditure, but it is a responsibility from which you cannot run. The promotion of healthy lifestyles, both in policy and practice, must be an important plank of your administration. A government that promotes healthy lifestyles realizes positive spin-offs for the agriculture sector, the rural sector, national productivity and the economy.

In many of our Caribbean jurisdictions, mental health is an often-neglected component of the public health system. In some of our countries, mental illness carries with it an unfortunate stigma. Regrettably, people who suffer from mental illness are sometimes seen as weak or victims of some unfortunate mishap. This prevents mental illness from being treated the way many other illnesses are addressed by our health system. Also, depression and anxiety often go untreated, leading to more serious and debilitating problems. Your government must do all within its power to increase access to mental health care, particularly at the community level. Government, as one of the largest employers on the island, should demonstrate its sensitivity to this issue by instituting an employee assistance programme to provide support to public officers who are experiencing emotional, financial or other stresses that may be negatively impacting their ability to function at work. During my tenure as minister for the public service, we established such a programme for public officers and not only was the programme soon oversubscribed, but the responses of those who used the confidential, professional services were overwhelmingly positive. I highly recommend it, but even more importantly, strongly encourage you as prime minister to treat the mental health of your citizens with the seriousness it deserves.

Social safety nets must be provided to cater to the vulnerable and disadvantaged. These should be based on means and economic circumstance, not political affiliation. Safety nets must be targeted, to ensure adequate coverage of those who require support, without wastage of scarce resources on those who do not need assistance. As much as possible, your goal should be to break the cycle of inter-generational poverty, with programmes that are developmental as well as supportive.

Appropriate and affordable housing programmes are important and housing developments should be undertaken with a view toward creating safe, interactive and healthy communities. Means testing should be employed when government undertakes housing developments for the vulnerable and disadvantaged to ensure that those who require the support are the ones who get it.

In crafting your social policy, attention must be paid to programmes that provide the necessary assistance to single mothers, the elderly, the physically challenged and youth-at-risk. A society is only as strong as its most vulnerable members. Your success will be measured not solely in terms of economic viability, but also by how you improve the key social indicators. Empirical data and evidence are your allies, regardless how unflattering a picture they may paint. You should adopt an evidence-based culture to help you identify where assistance is necessary, to determine the efficacy of the support that your government is providing, and to inform any necessary adjustments that will make it possible for the interventions to have the desired impact.

NATURAL RESOURCE MANAGEMENT

The environment is the third, and unfortunately most often neglected pillar of sustainable development. It is the substrate that feeds economic development. A weak or ailing environment renders economic development agendas unsustainable and creates anxiety and vulnerability that weaken social platforms.

For natural resource management to be effective, it must be given the necessary administrative support. It makes sense to establish a distinct ministry with responsibility for the environment or natural resource management. All the agencies that are responsible for the myriad elements of environmental management should be placed in this ministry. This is important, and it will significantly reduce the potential for duplication and conflict. Too often, governments treat environmental management as an afterthought and they append this responsibility to some other major portfolio. The result is the minister responsible usually relegates that part of his or her portfolio to secondary importance. When the environment is neglected, the economy and the country suffer.

Natural resource management never succeeds if the government uses only a top-down approach.

Firstly, you will not have the necessary human resources to carry out effective environment policing. Secondly, if the citizens do not appreciate the importance of environmental protection, you will face an almost Sisyphean task. Therefore, effective public education and public relations are important tools in your arsenal and you should use them.

Environmental management cannot be the sole preserve of the Ministry of the Environment. In much the same way that every ministry understands its role in stimulating economic development, every agency must embrace the responsibility for managing our natural assets. The serious threat now posed by climate change makes it essential that environmental management and climate change adaptation are mainstreamed into the work of every government agency. The Department of Planning and the Ministry of Finance must be seized of the environmental challenges facing the country and ensure that in both development planning and the allocation of financial resources, environmental issues are given adequate consideration.

There must be close coordination between the Physical Planning Department and the Ministry of the Environment because this is usually where many of the national environmental challenges originate. The Physical Planning Department should be staffed with competent people, who are allowed to operate without political interference.

Their role is to use their expertise, experience and sound judgement to deliberate on proposed infrastructure developments and determine the conditions under which these developments should be allowed to proceed. The Department of Planning must always factor environmental considerations in formulating the medium and long-term development strategies for the country. To do otherwise would be unsustainable and counter-productive.

Your government will need the support of non-governmental organizations (NGOs) and civil society organizations (CSOs) in addressing the challenges of environmental management. Sometimes, this relationship will become strained. However, it should never be allowed to descend to acrimony. It is important that you always keep the doors of dialogue open. You will find that most times, although the priorities and pathways may be different, the goals are not.

The water sector is one to which you should pay very close attention. Almost every Caribbean island experiences challenges with the availability of water and the efficient distribution of potable water to its citizens. These problems are often worsened by poor land use and bad management of watersheds. Unfortunately, climate change, through more frequent flooding, longer drought periods, more intense hurricanes that damage water infrastructure, and sea level rise-induced saline water intrusion that compromises groundwater sources, will negatively impact the water sector. Because the water sector is so vital to the socio-economic development of your country, I would recommend that you ensure the requisite institutional structures are in place to facilitate sound governance in this sector and the sustainable management of your critical water resources. Policies that regulate development and activities in proximity to water sources, encourage water storage, rainwater harvesting and promote the use of rainwater for non-essential purposes are highly recommended in any small island developing State.

Finally, on the issue of water, do not neglect the equally critical area of wastewater management. This can have serious implications for public health, tourism and environmental integrity.

CLIMATE CHANGE

There are few, if any, issues that pose as great a threat to your country as climate change. Unfortunately, all small island developing States (SIDS) around the world, for the foreseeable future, will have to cope with and adapt to the negative effects of climate change.

The impacts of climate change will manifest in several forms – more frequent flooding, prolonged droughts, sea level rise, the acidification of oceans and the consequential impacts on fisheries and marine ecosystems, the public health threat posed by new vector-borne diseases, and the salinization of ground water sources, to name a few. Even more menacingly, climate change will cause an intensification of hurricanes and storms, and we have already seen the devastation that strong hurricanes can bring to a Caribbean island State. We need look no further than the effect of Hurricane Gilbert on Jamaica, Hurricane Ivan on Grenada, Hurricane Irma on the British Virgin Islands, Antigua and Barbuda and Anguilla, and Hurricane Maria on Dominica and Puerto Rico to see how a Caribbean country and its people can be rendered completely helpless by a direct hit from a hurricane.

Therefore, your government must integrate planning for climate change in every sphere of its operations. One of the places to start is the Physical Planning Department. A firm decision must be taken on the types of infrastructure developments that are approved and allowed in areas that are prone to storm surges and extreme flooding. While a large hotel or a high density, high-value residential complex on a beachfront may have strong political and public relations appeal, this type of development will be among those most in peril when a hurricane strikes your country. Your government, like every other government in a small island developing State, must establish new planning regulations and guidelines to increase your country's resilience to the impacts of climate change. I would also recommend the creation of a land use plan, if one does not already exist, informed by climate change modelling data, which stipulates the types of development that may take place in the different parts of your country. You need to minimize, as best you can, unplanned developments that result in indiscriminate land clearing, deforestation, degradation of watersheds, obstruction of water courses, destruction of mangroves and wetlands and the other man-made problems that exacerbate the impacts of climate change.

The effects of climate change can be very devastating to lives and livelihoods in your country. Therefore, it would be wise to invest in a comprehensive national early warning system, to allow you to be able to evacuate residents from areas likely to be severely impacted by an extreme weather event.

Because of your country's geography and the fact that elevated sea surface temperatures brought on by climate change are causing hurricanes to become more intense, there is a high probability, unfortunately, that at some point, your country will be hit by a major tropical storm or hurricane. This means that your emergency management mechanism must always be in a state of preparedness. To be effective, emergency response and management systems must be functional at the community level, with strong coordination at the national level. Clear, unambiguous communication is vital, both before and after an emergency. I cannot overstate the importance of having strong managers, with good communication skills, heading your emergency management operations at all levels. It is my hope that these systems will not be tested during your tenure, but the probability of this happening, because of climate change, is becoming more likely and they must be able to respond effectively to save lives and protect livelihoods.

Public education is one of the most important tools in your arsenal for dealing with climate change. The Caribbean demonstrated the value of a grassroots-driven public education programme with its '1.5 to Stay Alive' media campaign in the build-up to negotiations on the Paris Agreement on climate change in 2015. This campaign, in which I was integrally involved, engaged youth groups, artists and journalists to spread the word on the need for decisive action on climate change. There are important lessons here for your administration, not just in the climate change arena. Your citizens are more likely to heed a call and assimilate a message when it is also being spread by people with whom they can more readily identify.

While climate change presents an existential threat to your country, it also provides an opportunity. The opportunity lies in your ability to leverage your position as a small island developing State to mobilize important financial and technical resources for the myriad sectors that are impacted by climate change. This will require very close coordination among your Ministry of External Affairs, Ministry of Finance and Ministry of the Environment. Robust, accurate and up-to-date empirical data will be a very valuable asset in helping you to make your case for support and you should ensure that this is understood by your government agencies. Accessing climate finance can be a difficult and onerous task. However, given the importance of these funds in helping you build climate resilience, it would be wise to give this issue serious attention.

The other opportunity provided by climate change is to facilitate a transition of your economy away from the use of fossil fuels in the energy and transport sectors to a new vibrant, sustainable energy sector that has tremendous transformative potential. The renewable energy sector will attract new investments and create new jobs. It will also lower and stabilize energy prices, which will have positive repercussions on your economic sectors.

Finally, as a leader of a small island developing State you have a responsibility to advocate on behalf of all SIDS for more decisive and urgent action to assist climate-vulnerable countries like yours increase their resilience to extreme weather events and adapt to the effects of climate change. Like all SIDS, your country is at the mercy of a dangerous threat that it did not create and to which it did not contribute. You must use every opportunity at your disposal to impress on the international community, particularly the developed countries that are the major emitters of greenhouse gases, the need for urgent action to reverse the effects of climate change. You must highlight the fact that your acute vulnerability to the wide-ranging impacts of climate change requires greater sensitivity on the part of development partners to the types and levels of support that they provide and the conditions to which they attach this assistance.

HERITAGE, ARTS & CULTURE

A country that does not value its heritage or does not support its culture and the arts has no true sense of purpose or identity. You should not commit the cardinal sin of which some governments are guilty of not providing sufficient support to heritage protection and the development of the arts and culture. You will find that investments in these areas will pay off handsomely in stimulating economic development and strengthening the social fabric of the country.

It is important that you demonstrate public appreciation for your exemplary citizens. One way to do this is by recognizing those unsung heroes whose sweat and tears built the nation that you now lead. The youth need to understand that they are standing on the shoulders of many local giants who made possible the quality of life and the level of development they now enjoy. This will cause them to develop a healthier appreciation of their past and the role that they in turn must play in contributing to national development. It also gives them the comfort that one day, they too will be recognized and appreciated for the work that they have done. This is important. You may wish to establish a mechanism for naming national assets after outstanding citizens, past and present, who have contributed to development. Schools, health facilities, community centres, roads, bridges and public libraries should all be named after the men and women who played a part in the growth of the nation. This is an excellent opportunity to bring your country together in a national, non-partisan manner.

The artists must feel that you value and appreciate their contribution to the socio-economic development of the country. For this to happen, you must ensure that arts and culture are treated with respect by your government. Training opportunities should be provided for artists to expand their skills. Schools should be made to incorporate arts programmes into the curriculum. Attention should be paid to the facilities and conditions under which local artists perform to ensure they are acceptable and accessible. Whenever possible, functions hosted by your government should include paid performances by local artists, and public spaces should be decorated with local art and craft. Whenever practicable, the design of public buildings should incorporate vernacular architectural elements. The creative industries represent a potentially lucrative form of economic activity, which will allow you to generate national wealth, create new avenues for employment, and instil national pride.

The schools need to teach the history of your country, at all levels of the education system. If there is no national museum and art gallery, constructing one should be one of your administration's priorities.

As much as possible, you should incorporate indigenous and traditional knowledge into decision-making. Caribbean societies have inherited a treasure trove of knowledge from their ancestors on everything from agriculture to architecture. Yet we continue to ignore these rich insights in favour of imported and sometimes inappropriate techniques, many of which have not been tried or tested in our environments. A blend of local knowledge with modern technology and best practice will result in solutions that are better suited and adapted for the problems of the country and will go a long way toward ensuring the sustainability of the development efforts.

The prime minister has a responsibility to lead the fight to preserve the country's heritage. You are the prime custodian of your country's patrimony. If you demonstrate that you place a high value on it, you will send a strong signal to investors about the types of investments you wish to see in your country and the way your national assets and resources should be treated. You will also be saying unequivocally that you will defend the rights of your citizens in your country in all areas, from labour laws to cultural identity. Do not shirk that responsibility.

NATIONAL SECURITY

Perhaps the single most important responsibility with which you have been entrusted as prime minister is that of keeping your citizens safe and your country secure. Nothing will imperil your economic development prospects or drive investors away faster than an unsafe country. Your citizens will quickly forget all the benefits that they derive from your administration if they feel that criminal activity is out of control in their communities.

There are many elements to preserving law and order in your country. Most administrations focus primarily on 'boots on the street', but this is only one of the areas to which you must pay attention. If you have inherited a serious crime problem, the electorate will want to see improvements within a short space of time. While you must work assiduously to make the country more secure, you must recognize that short-term actions will not solve problems that are deep-rooted and complex.

You should assess your justice system to ensure that it is working efficiently. Citizens must have confidence in its ability to dispense justice speedily and fairly. Where laws need to be amended or modernized, make this a priority. If you need to strengthen your Department of Legislative Drafting and your Crown Prosecution Office, do so. The electorate does not have patience for excuses about problems that are within your purview to resolve.

Your police force must be properly resourced. Crime fighting is a sophisticated science and you must have the appropriate tools and competences to do it effectively. Intelligence gathering is critical, for both crime prevention and crime solving. Therefore, an intelligence unit, supported by a secure intelligence management database system, is an important component of your national security apparatus.

The police force must cultivate a good relationship with the community that it serves. Community policing should be a major element of your crime fighting strategy. Citizens must be engaged and feel invested in keeping their communities safe. They must also feel comfortable and safe sharing information with the police.

Technology plays a very important role in solving crimes, so investments in closed-caption television, a command and control system, automatic fingerprint identification, and a central electronic database, if these do not exist, would be prudent. Although the initial investment may appear daunting, the return on that investment is significant and manifold.

You should also pay close attention to the organization and management of your police force. Areas such as human resource management, media and public relations, and financial management are very important for the effective functioning of the police force. These functions should be carried out by trained, competent professionals. Strangely, they are often overlooked or minimized.

Those are some of the immediate, short-term solutions. But there are longer-term measures that you will need to employ to ensure that gradually you significantly reduce the crime problem in your country. One of these involves education and providing better learning opportunities for your citizens, from cradle to grave. Again, I cannot over-emphasize the importance of good early childhood development programmes, particularly for children in high-risk situations. Your government should develop and implement a comprehensive programme for vulnerable youth that seeks to reduce the risk factors and provide them with better options.

Parental skills training is another area that you should target. The implementation of programmes that mentor parents, particularly young parents, so that they can inculcate positive values in their children and teach them skills in conflict resolution by non-violent means is critical.

The justice system must be more adaptable in dealing with young offenders. Diversion programmes that prevent the early criminalization of young people are important. There are too few non-custodial options available. Also, there is a serious need for remedial and re-integration programmes to prevent the vexing issue of recidivism. These are all issues to which you must attend.

Finally, your administration must demonstrate that it truly has a zero tolerance for crime of all types, regardless the perpetrator. This should start with the simpler crimes like littering and disorderly conduct. It should encompass the prosecution of traffic offenses, which can help minimize damage to limb and life. Moreover, it must extend to white-collar crime.

Cynicism has grown in many societies that only 'certain' types of people get arrested and go to jail. Conviction and incarceration appear to be correlated with economic means. You must demonstrate unequivocally that this is not the case and that justice under your watch is indeed blind. As prime minister, you must signal that acts of corruption and illegality will be dealt with appropriately and decisively, particularly within the ranks of your administration.

THE YOUTH

Unfortunately, many administrations state that youth engagement and development is an integral component of their agenda, but pursue actions that suggest otherwise. Too often, the government's idea of youth engagement consists of token actions, such as appointing a youth representative to the board of directors of some statutory agencies, or establishing a Ministry of Youth but not giving it the necessary human or financial resources to carry out an effective youth development programme.

There is ample evidence, empirical and otherwise, that investing in youth development has both immediate and long-term benefits. Caribbean youth (Cunningham et al. 2008) have been shown to be subject to five major risks, namely (i) youth unemployment, (ii) adolescent pregnancy, (iii) reproductive health and HIV/AIDS, (iv) school drop-out, and (v) crime, violence and drug abuse. To mitigate these risks, certain interventions have been recommended. They are (i) investing in early childhood development programmes, (ii) ensuring youth complete secondary education, (iii) supporting effective parenting programmes, (iv) establishing systems to collect and analyse data on youth, (v) providing youth with incentives to avoid risky behaviour, (vi) making strategic investments in high violence communities to make them safe, and (vii) undertaking media campaigns to spread anti-violence messages. These investments have all been shown to positively impact on the gross domestic product of Caribbean countries (CARICOM Secretariat 2010), providing further proof that strategic support for youth benefits the economy.

But it is not only at-risk youth who need the support of your government. Regrettably, many governments fall victim to the paranoia that youth are a problematic demographic. They are not. Most youth are stable, well-adjusted and productive. Your administration needs to provide incentives to stimulate and nurture youth entrepreneurship. The creative industries like music, theatre, art, craft, graphic design, fashion, publishing, software development and video gaming hold tremendous potential for generating new wealth and creating new spheres of economic activity, particularly for youth, who normally dominate these industries. Training opportunities must be provided to help young people develop and expand their skills in these areas. Moreover, a support framework should be established that will allow skilled, competent young people to establish enterprises and market their products and services to a global audience.

Youth need to be encouraged to work together to achieve shared objectives. This means your government should actively support the formation of youth groups at the community and national levels. If possible, assistance should be provided to accredited and registered groups to facilitate the administrative functions of these groups. The groups should also be allowed to use public buildings, such as community centres, to host their meetings. A mechanism should be created to allow youth groups to participate meaningfully in decision-making and governance at the local government and national levels.

Sporting endeavour is another area where youth excel and your government must demonstrate its support. This can be done in several ways, such as (i) actively and aggressively identifying athletic scholarships for aspiring young athletes, (ii) providing support for sports clubs, particularly with physical locations for club offices and meetings, (iii) maintaining an active school sports programme, (iv) using your national television station and communication infrastructure to provide coverage of sporting activity in the country, (v) making medical insurance coverage available for all athletes who have been selected to represent their country, (vi) supporting an elite athletes programme, and (vii) ensuring that sporting infrastructure at the community and national levels is adequate, accessible and always properly maintained.

THE PUBLIC SERVICE

The public service is the machinery that allows you to manage the affairs of your government. It comprises the civil service, the police force, teaching service, fire service, prisons service, doctors, and nurses. It is a large, bureaucratic machinery that does not respond very well to sudden changes in direction or modus operandi. You must understand the public service if you wish to work effectively with it.

The public service is expected to serve the government of the day impartially and to the best of its ability. The public service is supposed to operate in a politically neutral manner and you, in turn, are supposed to keep it insulated from political interference. This is important. You should resist the temptation to populate the public service with political operatives. This does not suggest that competent persons from outside the public service should not be appointed to positions within the service. However, once appointed, every public officer has a responsibility to operate in a non-partisan manner and to maintain the highest levels of professional integrity.

One of the most often heard complaints about the public service relates to its efficiency and productivity. Although governments are quick to criticize the public service, very few ever do anything to address the problems. If you wish to improve something, you must first be able to measure it. Therefore, I would recommend that you spend some time developing appropriate indicators to measure the performance of the public service, particularly the specialized agencies. These indicators should come out of a consultative process that also involves public officers and their trade unions. After you have done this, establish the benchmarks for performance and an appropriate penalties and rewards system.

You should ensure that the performance management tools that are being used are relevant and effective. There must be clarity in the functions that your officers are expected to perform, and they must understand their responsibilities.

Very often, the organizational structures in the public service are static. This rigidity results in agencies that cannot respond to the changing needs of the environment in which they operate and the clients whom they serve. Moreover, business processes are usually long, redundant, antiquated and linear, making very little use of technology. If you are serious about making your public service more efficient, and I expect that this will be high on your agenda, then focus on improving business services and making use of technology to interconnect agencies and functions.

Goal-setting and robust monitoring and evaluation of performance are very important. It is very easy for government agencies to appear very busy, even overwhelmed, with work and still achieve nothing of substance. Every public service agency must be clear on its role in achieving the targets and goals set by your administration. The permanent secretaries are your accounting officers and you must ensure that they are indeed held accountable for the performance of their departments. Your administration's primary goal must be to get the public service to operate as a cohesive, responsive, dynamic structure.

The fast pace with which the world is changing, the tremendous volume of new information that is being generated, and the dramatic impact that technology is having on our lives, require that you invest in the continuous training and development of your public officers. Fortunately, technological advances now obviate the need for officers to travel overseas for all training. Most training can now be delivered remotely. Therefore, any investment in the delivery of relevant training to public officers is sound and will allow you to cultivate a public service that is productive, effective, dynamic and efficient.

EXTERNAL RELATIONS

The words of the popular folk song inform us that 'no man is an island, no man stands alone'. However, no island should stand alone. Your government must cultivate relationships with development partners and allied governments to assist with the execution of the development agenda.

Overseas missions have often been maligned for the high cost associated with running them. This criticism is often born out of a misunderstanding of the role of these missions and their poor utilization by the government. Your overseas missions are important representatives of your government in strategic geographic locations around the world and they have critical roles to play in helping you mobilize support for your national programmes and ensuring that you have allies in critical negotiating arenas. However, for them to discharge these important responsibilities they must be populated with skilled individuals.

The practice of many governments is to use their overseas missions to reward political favours of some of their high level influential supporters. It is not unusual for ambassadors or high commissioners to be selected from either losing election candidates of the ruling party or high-ranking members of the party's executive. Where these individuals have the requisite skills, experience, temperament and competences, there is little harm in making such an appointment. However, when the proposed head of mission has nothing to suggest the ability to function at the highest levels in a senior diplomatic position in a foreign country, you are doing your country significant harm by making such an appointment. An engaged overseas mission, headed by a competent chef de mission, with clear directions and support from capital, is a tremendous asset to your government. Do not rob yourself of this important tool by sacrificing competence at the altar of political expediency.

Your overseas missions and representatives are your face to the international community and your liaison with the countries that are your closest developmental allies. Always ensure that appointments to these missions are public knowledge and that the persons chosen to represent your country overseas, particularly in senior diplomatic positions, are of the highest integrity.

You should position your administration to take maximum advantage of any opportunities provided by development partners with mandates that align with your national goals. My most useful advice to you in this area is that you should clearly define your development agenda before you engage with these partners. You will find that the time taken to determine your national priorities and to identify the areas in which development partners may assist, based on their mandate and the resources at their disposal, will enhance your reputation with these agencies, as well as ensure that the support they provide is relevant and congruent with your needs.

Too often, governments march to the beat of the drum of development partners and implement projects that are the priorities of these agencies and not necessarily of the government. I would recommend that you assign your development planning agency the task of articulating a comprehensive medium-term national development strategy (in consultation with all relevant stakeholders), if one does not already exist. Immediately the cabinet has approved this strategy, you should convene a major development partner conference, where you invite all the major donor agencies to receive the strategy and initiate discussions on areas where they may be able to assist. This is the process that I employed in mobilising technical and financial support for an ambitious renewable energy programme in my country and not only did it yield significant positive results, but the development partners were highly supportive of the approach because it showed focus and clarity of purpose on the part of the government and it removed the possibility of duplication and wasted effort.

The Department of Planning and the Ministry of External Affairs will play important roles in resource mobilization in the international community, so you must ensure they are properly resourced, work closely together and are sharply focused on the development imperatives of the country.

You should make optimal use of the participation of your ministers and ambassadors in international meetings to generate support for your negotiating positions and for your development agenda. These international fora provide valuable opportunities for the high-level representatives of your country to interact with their peers from countries that can provide assistance. Consequently, these occasions should not be wasted.

An important but overlooked development partner, with a strong commitment to the advancement of your country, is the large population of trained and skilled persons who reside in the diaspora. This pool of talented and resourceful individuals, most of whom retain very strong attachments and interest in the land of their birth, is very willing and able to contribute to the social, economic, environmental, and cultural development of the country. Your government should reach out to the diaspora and actively seek to engage it in the promotion and implementation of the development agenda.

SOCIAL PARTNERSHIPS

To function effectively in government, and more importantly, for you to be successful as a prime minister, you must nurture meaningful relationships with the social partners. After all, the definition of democracy is 'government of the people, for the people, by the people'. It would be very arrogant and dangerous for you to believe that residing within your cabinet is the totality of the brain trust necessary to manage the country. Equally, it would be foolhardy of you to think that you can run your government effectively without the support of civil society.

A successful prime minister is one who learns very quickly the importance of sharing the responsibility of governance and the need for empowering others to shoulder that burden.

So, who are the social partners with whom your government should forge relationships? There are several. The trade unions are important, particularly to develop a common understanding of the economic and social challenges faced by workers and the actions that must be taken to overcome these challenges, while simultaneously increasing the competitiveness and productivity of the workforce. There is the business community, which must work together with the government to stimulate increased economic activity and generate additional employment. There is the farming and fishing community, which is very important for achieving food security and supporting the growth and development of the rural economy. Youth groups are important social partners for your government. They provide you with a means of determining the priorities and aspirations of young people and ensuring that the policies and programmes implemented by your government are youth-friendly and youth-positive.

While your government is expected to maintain a separation between church and state, it cannot overlook the importance of faith-based organizations in helping to strengthen the social fabric of the country and instilling the values necessary for a responsible and respectful citizenry. Community-based organizations can reach and touch citizens in their communities and in their homes. Therefore, they are critical allies in helping to develop community spirit and individual responsibility to solve local problems.

Environmental organizations must be encouraged because they are important and reliable partners in natural resource management and environmental protection.

Each of these social partnerships must be developed and nurtured by your government, however and whenever possible. Do not use their formation as a photo opportunity to suggest to the nation that your government is serious about partnerships with civil society, only to never meet with them again during your term of office. Ideally, your government should aim to meet with its social partners at least once a year to discuss issues of mutual concern, assess the effectiveness of the partnership and agree on priorities for the coming year.

As with all partnerships, there will be disagreements along the way. Partnership is not synonymous with unequivocal loyalty. When and where disagreements occur between the policy direction of your government and the objectives and opinions of your social partner, you should always seek to resolve these internally and amicably. One of your important roles as prime minister is that of prime mediator. You should always try to view the issue from the other perspective. This does not imply that you should always look to acquiesce. What it means is that you should always seek a solution that is mutually beneficial. However, when it is not possible to arrive at a solution that is satisfactory to both (or all) parties, then you will have to do what you were elected to – make the decision that is in the best interest of the country. Hopefully, the occasions when a compromise cannot be reached will be few and far between.

THE BUDGET

The preparation of the annual Estimates of Expenditure and Revenue, also known as the budget, is not simply a numbers exercise. The budget and the accompanying policy statement send a strong signal about the priorities of your administration and the policies you intend to pursue during the coming year to address the important economic, social and environmental issues confronting your administration and the country. The budget is highly anticipated by the local business community, foreign investors, the banking sector, international development partners and other local stakeholders who want to see what fiscal adjustments will be made, whether any new government revenue measures or taxes will be implemented, and which sectors will benefit from new programmes or additional allocations of funding.

Because of its importance to the economy and the development trajectory of the country, the budget should be viewed as a tool to make yearly strategic adjustments to steer the country in the direction you set at the beginning of your term of office. It should not be treated as a series of annual ad hoc, disjointed interventions that are primarily focused on fire-fighting and responding to short-term problems. The budget must be strategic in orientation and visionary in approach. It should purposefully guide the country in the direction in which your administration wishes it to go.

As much as possible, the preparation of the budget should involve extensive discussions with public and private sector agencies. Your public sector departments should be asked to prepare 5-year, or at least 3-year, budgets that identify the capital investments and the programmes that they are seeking to implement. There should be full justifications for these interventions and, most importantly, the benefits that these interventions will bring to the respective sectors and the country. Private sector agencies, including non-governmental organizations and civil society organizations, should be asked to submit recommendations for the budget on areas where they believe government intervention or assistance is required.

The exercise of developing the budget is one that also speaks to discipline. The financial year begins and ends on the same fixed dates every year. Therefore, a serious, disciplined government submits its budget for debate in Parliament in advance of the end of the financial year. In that way, the operations of government are not affected because there is no parliamentary approval to spend. A responsible government also provides the opposition sufficient time and supporting material to engage in an informed, constructive debate on both the Estimates of Expenditure and Revenue and the policy statement. Anything less flies in the face of democracy and accountability and should not be a feature of your administration.

Finally, the budget debate should never be one of gamesmanship or one-upmanship. The electorate needs to receive a full accounting of how the funds allocated in the previous year's budget were used and digest an informed and civilized debate on what benefits and adjustments are anticipated from the measures and the programmes proposed in the current budget. A debate should be precisely what it means and implies – a formal discussion in which opposing positions are put forward and argued. The institution of Parliament is devalued when it is used as an election campaign platform. Every parliamentarian must be accorded respect and it is your role as prime minister to set the example for this and the responsibility of the Speaker of the House to ensure this.

THE POLICY AGENDA

The saying 'The best laid plans of mice and men often go awry' is very appropriate in relation to the policies and plans of a government. Your job as prime minister is to put systems and processes in place that will give your plans and policies every possible chance at success, and be ready to make the necessary adjustments when these plans stutter.

Because policy formulation starts in your cabinet, this is where you should first focus your attention. The cabinet secretariat must be given the responsibility and the resources to monitor the implementation of cabinet decisions by the respective ministries and to report back to the cabinet on the effectiveness and impact of the decisions. Too often, cabinets make decisions and never receive feedback from the line ministry or the affected agencies on the efficacy of the decision. In some instances, cabinet decisions are never implemented, and cabinet is none the wiser. The role of the cabinet secretariat should not merely be to process memoranda to cabinet and disseminate cabinet decisions to line ministries; it must also monitor the effectiveness and impact of these decisions.

I would advise that you have semi-annual implementation review meetings with all your ministries. In these sessions, each ministry, headed by the minister and the permanent secretary, should present to you and the cabinet its achievements, based on the budget (and the accompanying work programme) that was passed in Parliament during the debate on the Appropriation Bill. These implementation review meetings should assess the success of the respective ministries in achieving their indicators and meeting their goals. They should not fall into the trap of measuring what percentage of the funds originally allocated has been spent by the ministry. This flawed metric, which is too often the focus of the Ministry of Finance, shifts the emphasis on spending money instead of achieving results. The semi-annual budget review exercise forms part of the goal-setting and performance-measuring process that I indicated earlier was an essential component of the results-based culture you need to establish among your ministers.

Whenever and wherever possible, government agencies should be encouraged to work together to address issues. While, for accounting purposes, only one ministry can have responsibility for a project, it is rare that a ministry, on its own, can completely solve the problem that a project or initiative seeks to address. Your government must promote inter-agency collaboration; the impact will be greater, more comprehensive and the results more enduring.

Often, there are structural impediments that make it difficult for programmes to be implemented efficiently. Where and when these exist, deal with them. Causing the sort of transformational change with which you want your administration to be associated will require you to do things differently and decisively. It was Albert Einstein who told us that 'we cannot solve problems using the same thinking that created the problem'. Yet, too often, we ignore this wisdom.

Be bold but smart in your approach. Address the short term while always planning for the long term. Yours is a small island developing State, with multiple challenges born out of physical size, geography, market size and a limited resource base. You must devise solutions that work for you. You should use your scarce assets prudently because you cannot afford the luxury of wasted resources or time. Ironically, your small size is also an asset. It allows you to be able to connect with, and reach, every nook and cranny of your country and almost every resident without too much effort. Use this to your advantage.

THE PARLIAMENT

Parliament is where laws are passed and amended. It is where government spending gets approved. It should also be where the work of the executive branch of the government is assessed and where the issues that affect the country and its citizenry are discussed and debated. It is that sacred place where the representatives of the people protect and defend the rights of the people they have been elected to serve.

Sadly, save for the first two functions, our parliaments seldom live up to their responsibility. Because there is very little, if any, separation between the executive and the legislative branches, Parliament is unable to objectively appraise the work of the executive. This is a serious deficiency, as it removes the medium for holding the executive branch accountable for its stewardship of the country. In effect, the majority of the members of Parliament, under our systems, have the responsibility to debate legislation that they have already discussed and approved in cabinet, review audit reports on the performance of the ministries they lead, and approve bills to provide funding for programmes that they will implement in their ministries. Those are not ideal conditions to ensure objective and effective parliamentary oversight.

Another regrettable shortcoming of Parliament is the paucity of informed debate on the major issues. It is only when the Estimates of Expenditure or a new major law is being debated that parliamentarians will come close to having a discussion on the critical topics that impinge on development. In short, Parliament is often viewed and treated by government MPs as a chore to be dispensed with; something that sometimes gets in the way of 'the real work' of government, that of being a minister. As the prime minister, who derives authority from the fact that you enjoy the support and confidence of the majority of the people who sit in the Parliament (not the cabinet), you must change this perception.

One of the early things you should do, if it has not yet been undertaken, is to embark on the modernization of your Constitution so that it provides a better and more appropriate framework for good governance and importantly, strengthens the Parliament so that it can better and more authoritatively appraise the work of the executive. This will not always be a popular decision, particularly among some of your colleagues, because the status quo is comfortable, safe and reduces the burden of accountability.

You should also insist that every minister must prepare an annual report of the work of his or her ministry, which must be tabled in Parliament during the debate on the Estimates of Expenditure. There should be a permanent record of the performance of your ministers, and the Parliament must be given an opportunity to assess the effectiveness of their stewardship.

Another neglected instrument for accountability is the report of the director of audit on the operations of government. Often, these reports are not up-to-date and when they do come to Parliament, they are not for the current period. If the audit reports are in arrears, you should provide the Office of the Director of Audit with the necessary resources to complete all outstanding government audits. After they have been completed, these reports should be subjected to scrutiny by the Parliament. The work of the Public Accounts Committee is very important in this regard and this committee should use its authority to invite ministers, permanent secretaries and other relevant public officers to meet with it to discuss the issues raised in the audit report. Moreover, measures must be put in place to ensure that government ministries comply with the recommendations of the director of audit.

As I have alluded to earlier, for parliamentary debates to be meaningful and productive, they should follow the format of a debate. For this to happen, certain traditions must be respected, such as making information on the subject that is being debated available to both parties, with sufficient time to prepare for the debate. Bills, particularly those that are complex or long, should not have all their readings rushed through in one sitting of

Parliament. This prevents the proposed new legislation from getting the scrutiny and being subjected to the analysis that is necessary before passage. Also, the government should not use its majority in the Parliament to ignore useful or meaningful recommendations from the opposition for changes to be made to the bill or the motion being debated. Remember, this bill will become law not too long after it has been passed in Parliament, and it is better to get it right the first time, than to have to suffer through its defects and return to Parliament to amend it later.

The Parliament is a collection of honourable persons and it should live up to this expectation. Together with the presiding officer, you should ensure that your Parliament always upholds the finest democratic traditions.

MEMBERS OF PARLIAMENT

The responsibility of representing the people who voted you into office has been somewhat relegated in importance because of the hybridization of the Westminster model of government in our jurisdictions. The first and most important job of a member of Parliament (MP) is to provide the best possible representation for his or her constituents, both those who voted him or her into office and those who did not. The second important responsibility is to function as a member of the legislative branch of the government: someone who sits in the Parliament and passes laws that are in the best interests of the people, approves spending that is necessary for the operations of the government, and ensures that the policies of the executive arm of the government will place the country and its citizens on a positive, viable and sustainable development path. Unfortunately, because generally there is little separation between the legislative and the executive branches of government, the job of the member of Parliament who sits on the government's side in the Parliament is often secondary to the perceived more important and prestigious role of the minister, the person who presides over a ministry and is given funds and the authority to spend those funds.

I believe it is necessary to separate, as much as possible, the legislative and the executive branches of the government. This is where Constitution modernization comes in. However, even without this, the prime minister needs to give MPs - government and opposition, the tools and the resources to carry out their important roles as representatives of the people. For this to happen, a few things must occur. Firstly, a functioning local government system needs to be in place. The local government authorities should have their own allocation of funds, based on an annual submission to the Ministry of Finance of the proposed plans and programmes for the coming year. These submissions by the local government authorities should be debated and approved in Parliament during the debate on the Estimates of Expenditure. Each local government authority must work closely with the respective MP to execute plans, programmes and projects that benefit the residents of the constituency. MPs and constituencies must be empowered, legally and financially, to do some things on their own, unencumbered by the large State bureaucracy, but held accountable by the Parliament that gave them the authority.

It would be disingenuous to propose this solution without addressing the huge elephant in the room – the issue of remuneration and finances. One of the reasons government MPs expect to be appointed to the cabinet is for the better pay that attaches to the position of a minister over that of an

MP without a ministerial portfolio. My advice is that you should remove this discrepancy and allow MPs to be paid a salary that adequately compensates them for the important job for which they have been elected. If you provide MPs with the resources to discharge their responsibilities effectively at the constituency and parliamentary levels and you give yourself the latitude to appoint the most competent people to head your ministries, you will have a government that operates more efficiently and at closer to optimal levels on both the executive and legislative levels. This will have tremendous benefit economically and socially for your country. Moreover, empowering MPs and communities to take greater responsibility for the development of their constituency should result in a more engaged and responsible citizenry, better implementation rates of projects, and greater relevance of the initiatives undertaken by government on behalf of the people. In short, it is a win-win scenario.

Finally, a word of caution. The persons who have been elected to represent their respective constituencies in the House of Assembly are equal. Opposition MPs are as deserving of support and assistance for their constituency as government MPs. Do not starve a constituency of much-needed support because it is not represented by a member of your party.

YOUR POLITICAL PARTY

Very often, when a political party in a small island developing State transitions into government, many of the people who played an active role in the management of the affairs of the party and who were instrumental in orchestrating the victory of the party at the general election, assume positions in the new government. This creates a serious vacuum of leadership and resources within the party and its effectiveness and dynamism suffer. Therefore, one of your first actions after you have settled your new government is to ensure that your party has life and can function effectively while you hold the reins of power.

There are two elements of party structure that must be reinvigorated after a general election. The first is the constituency groups. The tendency is for these to lapse, some out of disappointment at not being able to win the seat they contested, others due to a sense of accomplishment at having waged a successful campaign and feeling that their work is finished until the next general election campaign. Your task, together with your chairman, general secretary and other ranking members of your party, will be to devise ways of keeping your party constituency structure intact and enthused. New talent must be introduced to keep the process of renewal going and to sustain the level of interest in the work of the group. Each constituency group must conduct a post-election analysis of the performance of the party and the candidate in the election in that constituency. Almost immediately the general election is over, the constituency group must understand that its role is to start preparations for the next general election. Voter registration is a continuous process and voter databases must be updated regularly. Voter education never stops.

The second party element that must be re-energized after the general election is the specialised organs and representatives – the youth arm, the women's arm, the farmers' group, the private sector group, labour relations, fraternal relations, and any other specialized groups, committees or representatives that exist in your party. These groups are important because they operate at a national level and allow you to monitor the vital signs of your party within key sectors and demographics.

Throughout your term of office in government, you should make a special effort to meet regularly with the constituency groups and the specialised organs and dialogue with them. It is important that the party members never lose touch, literally and figuratively, with their elected officials, and most importantly, with their political leader and prime minister. Remember, it is these individuals whose hard work got you elected into office. Neglect them at your peril.

As prime minister and political leader, you also must create opportunities for your party to remain apprised of the policies and programmes of your government. While I strongly advise against a direct involvement of the party in the operations of the government, the party cannot be kept in the dark or caught by surprise by executive decisions. My recommendation would be, at a minimum, for a quarterly engagement between your party hierarchy and your ministers, where issues may be clarified or discussions held on issues of national importance.

Ministers and members of Parliament must remain accessible to senior party officials during their term in office. The party is the medium that must keep the government anchored and provide feedback on its effectiveness and connectedness with the electorate. It is the organ that must defend the government on the ground against unwarranted criticism from opposition elements. Therefore, the members of the government cannot and must never appear aloof or indifferent to the party and must never treat party responsibilities like a burden or a nuisance. The onus is on you as the political leader to set the tone and the example in this area.

PUBLIC RELATIONS

Many governments put themselves under additional pressure because of an inability to communicate with the electorate what they are doing, what they have done and what they intend to do. The marketing of the goals and achievements of a government is a complex and important task. Many governments slowly start to lose popularity within the first year after a general election. Political parties quickly learn that there is a big difference between being in opposition and having the liberty and the latitude to criticize everything that the incumbent is doing, and being in office and having to deliver on the many promises that were made on the campaign trail, to an electorate that had been seduced into believing that all their problems would have been addressed by a new administration.

Therefore, an effective communications strategy and an efficient public relations machinery are essential if you want to slow down the attrition and convince the electorate that you are not only doing the best you can in the prevailing circumstances, but that no one else can do any better. You must stress to your ministers and your government MPs the importance of communication and of maintaining a cordial, respectful relationship with the media. This may not always be easy, but it is essential.

Two different sets of public relations mechanisms will be required, and you should not confuse, mix or interchange the two. There is the public relations that your political party must engage in to align itself with the positive work of the government and promote the achievements of the individual parliamentarians, particularly the initiatives that are being undertaken at the community level. There is also the public relations that the government must undertake to highlight and promote its programmes and achievements, and to educate the public about any new projects that are being pursued. For this, you will need separate and distinct communications apparatus. The prime minister's press secretary and the Government Information Service should not speak on behalf of your political party; that responsibility should fall to your party's public relations machinery and the members of your party's executive.

Do not overestimate the retention capacity of the citizenry. In other words, do not assume that because you have explained something once or twice that you never need to return to it. The most successful and best-known companies in the world spend millions of dollars every year on marketing, with carefully designed campaigns that are tailored to appeal to specific demographics, and vary according to the time of year or occasion. Why should you think that your government, which is trying to market the benefits of a new policy, programme or project that may not resonate with everyone, can do so successfully with just one or two public service announcements that are repeated a few times on radio and television? Or that a static hour-long television interview with a minister or a senior public officer can change the minds and attitudes of large numbers of people toward a subject? This deficiency becomes even more glaring in the present environment, where attention spans are shorter and there are so many other, more interesting television programmes and online videos competing for the attention of the viewer.

Your government communications department must be properly resourced with trained and experienced media personnel who understand the subtleties of information dissemination and who are comfortable communicating across multiple platforms and media. They must be encouraged to take a proactive approach to communicating the work of the government to the public. They should see their role as that of marketing agents for the government, who must package government news and information into attractive and dynamic content that is delivered to the audience over multiple media outlets, including all the social media platforms. Many political parties have lost a general election after having done impressive work in government during their term of office, simply because insufficient numbers of voters knew, remembered or understood the significance of the work they had done.

You should ensure that your party's public relations apparatus is functional from the day you assume office and insist that all ministers and government parliamentarians always make themselves fully accessible to the party's public relations officers. Each of your ministers should be required to put in place a functioning mechanism to provide the party's public relations machinery with information on the work being carried out by his or her department. Your party's public relations machinery should not go into hibernation after you have won the general election, to awaken and resurface just prior to the start of the next election campaign. By that time, it may be too late.

THE ELECTORATE

Remaining connected with the electorate is one of your most important goals during your term of office. It may sound simple and obvious, but it is easy for a prime minister, particularly a new one, who is inundated by a relentless torrent of urgent national issues, and travel duties that require frequent absences from the country, to have fewer opportunities to meet with the electorate in situ and, therefore, to be forced to rely increasingly on reports relayed by others. This cannot be your story.

You must understand the nuances and complexities of the society. You are the prime minister of everyone - the poor, the disenfranchised, the youth, the elderly, the farmers, the fishers, the hotel employees, the roadside vendors, the middle class, the business owners, the hoteliers, the taxi drivers, the environmentalists, the social activists, the artists and the public officers. Everyone is deserving of, and entitled to your attention. You must devise ways to interact with all the various demographics and interest groups to fully and clearly understand their problems and to work with them to fashion solutions.

As the prime minister and political leader of your party you have two very critical reasons to stay grounded and keep your finger on the pulse of the people. The first is you are now running a government that is formulating policies and implementing programmes that are expected to improve the quality of life of your citizens and place your country on a better and more sustainable development footing. There are two ways to determine whether your interventions are having the desired effect. There is the empirical data that your government agencies collect on key performance indicators, and there is also the critical qualitative evidence that you gather from talking and interacting with the people your programmes are intended to assist. If these people tell you that their situation has not improved, or life has become more challenging, you should not discount or diminish their claims simply because the information from your Statistics Department suggests otherwise. While I am a very strong proponent of the use of empirical data in decision making, this should never lead to the exclusion of qualitative information, the kind you gather from real-life encounters with a wide cross-section of your citizens.

The second reason involves your responsibility as the political leader of your party. You must ensure that the actions of your government and the measures you are implementing are not making you unpopular among the people who will have to judge your performance at the ballot box at the next general election. History is littered with examples of political parties that did all the right things in government to improve the metrics that the international financial institutions insist are the most important indicators of economic health, only to be resoundingly defeated at the next general election because they disconnected from the people and their policies and programmes worsened the lives of those they were meant to help.

Keeping yourself grounded is critical. This means regularly getting out of your office and going into the communities, sometimes unannounced and untethered from the constraints of your security detail, and mixing, listening, sharing and talking. It includes making unscheduled and unscripted visits to police stations, farms, fire stations, health centres and hospitals, roadside vendors, taxi stands and other areas where your citizens ply their trade and live their lives. It involves stepping away from the VIP section every so often, to sit and mingle with the general population at sporting and cultural events. These encounters will teach you more about life in the country under your administration than any set of statistical indices or commissioned reports.

You must ensure that your MPs keep in close contact with their constituents. Where MPs are also ministers, it is very easy for them to become consumed with their ministerial duties and with official travel, and consequently devote insufficient time to interacting with their constituents in the communities. The practice of reducing meetings with constituents to once-weekly clinics in a constituency office is risky. It robs the MP of the ability to obtain a feel for life in the constituency and to observe, at source, the issues affecting the residents. It is your responsibility as prime minister and political leader to constantly remind your MPs of the need to remain faithful to their responsibilities to their constituents.

You should cultivate a healthy and respectful relationship with the media. Not all of them will support you or approve of what you are doing, but that should not stop you from regularly engaging with them and having frank and informed discussions about your policies and objectives. You will not always agree with the media's assessment of your government or its actions, but disagreement should never degenerate to incivility or hostility. Holding the reins of power does not make you always right. It is extremely important that you listen. The ability to listen and absorb constructive feedback is one that some government politicians seem to lose very easily. Most importantly, do not ever believe that you are omnipotent, omniscient or infallible. You are human, and you will err. When you do, admit your mistake, apologize and learn the salient lessons from it.

YOUR JOURNEY

I hope I have convinced you that while running a government is not rocket science, it is also not a leisurely, late evening stroll along the beach. You must work at being a prime minister and at making your administration effective and successful. You will make mistakes, but you will learn on the job and, hopefully, you will get better with every new challenge you confront.

One of the serious challenges you will confront during your term of office is healing the nation after a divisive election campaign. You must emphasize to your team the importance of reaching out to all, regardless of political persuasion, and governing on behalf of all, regardless of voting preference. It is essential that the country works as one if you are to achieve the goals you set for your administration. This will not always be easy. Taking and keeping the moral high ground require effort and persistence.

Ensuring that all members of your team uphold the highest standards of political office must also be of utmost importance to you. Holding political office is a serious and important responsibility, to which you, your cabinet and your parliamentary colleagues must live up. It will be necessary that you establish with your colleagues from the outset what will not be tolerated in your administration so that everyone has a common understanding of the ethos of your government. No one, including you, should get a pass for illegal, unethical, corrupt or dishonest behaviour.

You must remember that during your term of office, you are always the prime minister. You can no longer speak in a personal capacity. There should never be an unguarded moment. There is no such thing as an 'off the record' remark.

You should recognize that the public has a right to information on what its government is doing. While there will be elements of your work that must remain confidential, appointments to public office, remuneration of public officials, disbursements of contracts, incentives to individuals and companies, and other activities that involve the use of State funds should not be kept secret from the public.

You are living in an era of instant information and widespread use of social media. This presents exciting opportunities for communication with your citizens, both resident and within the diaspora, of which you should avail yourself. An educated and informed electorate is much more likely to support the positive things that you do. However, you must also understand that instant communication and omnipresent social media is a sharp, double-edged sword. It means that anything negative or inappropriate that you do or say can be distributed to a global audience with hitherto unprecedented speed.

Unfortunately, your family will experience some discomfort because of your position as prime minister. It must be prepared for the occasional inconvenience. Very little that you or a close family member does or says from the day you become prime minister will be immune from public scrutiny. Appointments to a position of public office or the award of a contract to any member of your family for the supply of goods or services to government must come out of a competitive and transparent process. It does not matter how qualified the family member may be, you will not be able to convince anyone that a direct award of a job or a contract is not the result of political influence and does not constitute a conflict of interest at best or nepotism at worst.

These caveats notwithstanding, holding the office of head of government is one of the most prestigious and honourable positions anyone can have. You have been given a unique opportunity, enjoyed by very few, to make profound improvements to the quality of the lives of your fellow citizens and to positively impact the development prospects of your country. If you treat your job with the level of preparation, respect and seriousness that it deserves, you will etch your name in the annals of history of your country in a way few others can. Grasp the opportunity and do good with it.

EPILOGUE

Unfortunately, no incoming prime minister inherits a 'clean slate'. He or she may find a country with serious economic, social and environmental problems. It is likely that some of the citizens will be cynical, indifferent and reluctant to participate in the manner required to ensure the optimal use of human resources. There may be a high level of political polarization, particularly in the aftermath of the general election. Supporters of the defeated party may not all be in a conciliatory or cooperative mood. Even more importantly, the new parliamentary opposition may remain, for an extended period, in a defiant mode, refusing to engage in a constructive manner on the important challenges that require a common national understanding and response.

Any one of these scenarios will hinder the new prime minister and administration in their ability to govern effectively. A confluence of two or more will certainly conspire to make life very challenging for a new administration. It is not possible to put the country on pause and simply come in with a new team to do things better and differently immediately. Regrettably, it is not like the changeover of bands during a concert, when the stage handlers of the new band simply change the instruments and adjust the sound levels, and the members of the new band take their places behind their instruments and effortlessly produce the sweet melodies that the audience has paid for and is anticipating. It is more like the physician who must treat multiple ailments in a patient, while allowing that patient to go about his or her normal life with very little disruption.

Luckily, these problems are not insurmountable. If they were, there would be no point to this book. Dealing with them will take firmness and resolve. The new prime minister and administration must signal clearly and early that it will not be business as usual. Where there are tough decisions to be taken, the context to the problems must be explained, in as objective and understandable a manner possible. There is always the temptation for a new administration to remind the public, at every turn, of the failings of the previous administration. The fact that there was a change in government means that a majority of the public is already aware of these shortcomings. New administrations should not succumb to this temptation too often. Eventually, it has the opposite effect and destroys goodwill.

To win the trust of the people, the new government must shift its lens from viewing them as electorate to now seeing them as citizens. Governments are elected to serve all the people, not just those who voted for them. Consistency, fairness and transparency of actions are critical in winning and keeping the trust and confidence of the people. This will be important to secure the support required for executing the new development agenda and making some of the tough decisions that will be necessary.

The new administration must do all within its power to reduce the political polarization of the society by being more inclusive, more engaging and more open in its operations. The government cannot influence the posture that the opposition adopts. However, it can remove some of the excuses that the opposition normally provides for being confrontational, such as a lack of public information or an unwillingness on the part of the government to consult or engage constructively on matters of national significance. Sharing information with stakeholders does not diminish the capacity to govern or the authority to make decisions. On the contrary, it helps to reassure everyone that the proposed actions have been carefully deliberated.

Finally, if the new prime minister and the government are not able to inspire, then their term of office will be pedestrian, unambitious, ineffective and disappointing. The prime minister and the government should seek to motivate citizens to do better, to be better and to aim higher. They must convince everyone of the need to work together and channel their energies toward a common good. Most importantly, they must lead by example.

REFERENCES

CARICOM Secretariat, 2010. *Eye on the Future: Investing in Youth Now for Tomorrow's Community.* Report of the CARICOM Commission on Youth Development. CARICOM Secretariat, Guyana.

Cicero, Quintus Tullius, 2012. *How to Win an Election.* Princeton University Press

Cunningham, Wendy, Linda McGinnis, Rodrigo Garcia Verdu, Cornelia Tesliuc and Dorte Venner. 2008. *Youth at Risk in Latin America and the Caribbean: Understanding the Causes, Realizing the Potential.* World Bank, Washington, DC.

Gibson, Rowan. 1998. *Rethinking the Future: Rethinking Business Principles, Competition, Control and Complexity, Leadership Markets and the World.* Hodder & Stoughton, London.

McCain, Margaret N, and Fraser Mustard. 1999. *Reversing the real brain drain: early years study: Final Report.* Toronto: Canadian Institute of Advanced Research.

United Nations Environment Programme, 2011. *Towards a Green Economy: Pathways to Sustainable Development and Poverty Eradication – a Synthesis for Policy Makers.* UNEP.